#LIVELACROIX
lacroixwater.com

YUMMY YOGA

Playful Poses and Tasty Treats

By
JOY BAUER
MS, RDN, CDN

Photography by
BONNIE STEPHENS

Abrams Books for Young Readers · New York

Namaste xx Joy

Lift the flap to stretch your taste buds with a creamy treat!

HOLY BROCCOMOLE!

A delicious dip packed with vitamins *and* minerals.

BROCCOMOLE DIP

Makes about 2 cups

1 to 2 cups broccoli florets

2 ripe avocados, peeled and chopped

½ cup chopped tomatoes

2 to 4 tablespoons finely chopped red onion

2 tablespoons lime juice

½ teaspoon kosher salt

2 tablespoons chopped cilantro (optional)

1 garlic clove, finely chopped (optional)

Black pepper (optional)

Steam, microwave, or boil the broccoli in a small amount of water until it's very soft. Drain off all water.

Place the broccoli and avocados in a mixing bowl and mash with a fork until smooth.

Add the chopped tomatoes, onion, lime juice, and salt. Add the cilantro and garlic to the bowl if you wish. Mix until well combined. Season with a bit of additional salt and a sprinkle of pepper to taste.

Serve with raw broccoli florets, baby carrots, bell pepper sticks, or whole-grain crackers, and start dipping!

Welcome to YUMMY YOGA!

I'm a health expert, so it's my job to encourage you to nourish your body with feel-good food and exercise.

Healthy foods can be **fun** and delicious. Check out the eight easy recipes in this book, packed with vitamins, minerals, and fiber. There are also eight yoga positions to learn, which will help make you stronger, more flexible, calmer, and better balanced.

Doing yoga is super fun! It's what inspired my friend Bonnie to create amazing yoga sculptures made out of tasty food. Try copying the poses, and then get cooking in the kitchen with my Joy-full recipes.

Preparing **vegetables** and fruits in different ways can change the tastes and textures, giving them an entirely new look and feel. Sometimes it takes a few tastes before you start falling in love with a new food (even one you think you won't like!). Feel free to mix and match ingredients—be **creative**.

Now it's time to stretch your body *and* your taste buds for a happier, healthier you!

Namaste, *Joy*

P.S. When we practice yoga, we say "namaste" (nah-mah-STAY), which means "I see the best in you."

Always ask an adult for help, especially if you need to use a knife or the stove!

Look under the flap for a colorful veggie party!

and plenty of fiber, too!

HEART-Y ARTICHOKES, GREEN BEANS & LEEKS

Makes about 6 cups

WHAT YOU'LL NEED

2 tablespoons olive oil

2 tablespoons lemon juice

3 garlic cloves, finely chopped
   (or ¼ teaspoon garlic powder)

½ teaspoon kosher salt

¼ teaspoon black pepper

4 to 5 cups fresh green beans

One 14-ounce can quartered artichoke
   hearts, drained, rinsed, and patted dry

2 or 3 leeks, sliced and cleaned (use only
   the white and pale green parts)

Nonstick oil spray

½ cup pomegranate seeds

½ cup roasted pistachio nuts, shelled

HOW TO MAKE IT

Preheat the oven to 425°F. Combine the olive oil, lemon juice, garlic, salt, and pepper in a mixing bowl. Add the green beans, artichokes, and leeks. Stir to coat evenly.

Mist a baking sheet with oil spray and spread the mixture on the sheet in a single layer. Roast for about 20 to 25 minutes or until the vegetables are slightly browned and crispy. (I think they're extra delicious when the edges get super crisp!)

Remove from oven and garnish with the pomegranate seeds and pistachios.

TRIANGLE POSE
Helps make you flexible.

BERRY-BANANA SMOOTHIE

Makes about 3 cups

WHAT YOU'LL NEED

1 banana, fresh or frozen

2 cups sliced strawberries, fresh or frozen

¼ cup blueberries, fresh or frozen

1 cup fresh kale, stems removed

½ cup milk of choice (if using frozen fruit, may need to add a dash more milk)

3 to 5 ice cubes (optional, omit if using frozen fruit)

HOW TO MAKE IT

Place all the ingredients in a blender, and purée until smooth.

Handy hack: Pour any leftover smoothie into ice cube trays and freeze. Then, when you're ready to make more, toss your "smoothie cubes" into the blender with some milk, and purée.

LOTUS POSE
Great for calming your mind and body.

Take a peek under the flap for a berry delicious, vitamin-filled energy boost.

SIP-SIP-HOORAY!

A smoothie packed with noteworthy nutrients.

PLANK POSE
Perfect for strengthening your belly and back muscles!

CORN ON THE COB WITH A TWIST!

Makes 4 pieces

WHAT YOU'LL NEED

2 ears of corn, husks removed

2 limes, cut into quarters

2 to 3 tablespoons finely chopped cilantro

2 to 3 tablespoons grated Parmesan cheese

HOW TO MAKE IT

Snap both ears of corn in half. Bring a large pot of water to a boil, then add corn. Return the water to a boil for about 4 minutes, then carefully remove corn from the water with tongs.

Squeeze the juice of the limes over the corn. Sprinkle with cilantro and Parmesan cheese.

WARRIOR II POSE
Helps stretch out your legs and hips.

SWELL SHELLS & SUPER SPEARS

Makes about 17 cups

WHAT YOU'LL NEED

FOR THE PASTA
One 16-ounce box whole-grain pasta shells
2 tablespoons olive oil
¾ teaspoon garlic powder
½ teaspoon Kosher salt

FOR THE BROCCOLI
2 cups reduced-sodium broth
1 to 1½ pounds broccoli florets
Kosher salt and black pepper
⅔ cup grated Parmesan cheese

FOR THE ASPARAGUS
1 bunch fresh asparagus (tough ends removed)
2 tablespoons olive oil
½ teaspoon kosher salt

HOW TO MAKE IT

Cook the pasta al dente according to the package directions. Drain and add back to the pot, with the heat turned off. Mix in the olive oil, garlic powder, and salt. Cover and set aside.

While the pasta is cooking, prepare the broccoli: Add the broth to a large skillet and bring to a simmer over medium-high heat. Add the broccoli florets and cook for about 3 minutes, stirring occasionally.

Toss the cooked broccoli and the broth into the pot with the pasta until everything is combined. Mix in grated Parmesan cheese and season with extra salt, pepper, and a bit more garlic powder to taste.

To make the asparagus, preheat the oven to 400°F. Combine the asparagus with the olive oil in a bowl and toss. Spread the spears out on a baking sheet in a single layer and sprinkle with the salt. Roast for 20 to 25 minutes.

LEAN, GREEN VITAMIN MACHINE!

A delish dish with broccoli and asparagus.

Lift the flap for a tasty meal to tempt your tummy!

corn on the cob is oh-so-delicious!

Look under the flap—it's *time* for *lime*!

TREE POSE
Improves your balance.

POWER POPS

Makes 9 pops

WHAT YOU'LL NEED

1 cup carrot juice

2 cups sliced strawberries, fresh or frozen

¼ cup pink grapefruit juice

2 kiwis, peeled (plus 1 more kiwi, peeled and cut into 9 slices, for optional garnish)

2 tablespoons honey

HOW TO MAKE IT

Combine all the ingredients in a blender and purée until smooth. Pour the mixture into a set of ice pop molds, using about ⅓ cup mixture per pop. (Add a floating kiwi slice for decoration if you like.) Freeze until the pops are solid, at least 3 hours.

An alternative method if you don't have ice pop molds: Pour the mixture into small paper cups and wrap each top tightly with a piece of aluminum foil. Carefully poke a wooden popsicle stick through the foil to serve as a handle, making sure each stick is centered and straight, then freeze until solid.

POPSICLES WITH PIZZAZZ...

a fabulous frozen snack!

Look under the flap for a *meow*-wow of a treat!

CAT POSE

Purr-fect for warming up your spine.

MINI EGGPLANT PIZZAS

Makes about 12 slices

WHAT YOU'LL NEED

Nonstick oil spray

1 large unpeeled eggplant

1 to 2 tablespoons olive oil

Kosher salt and black pepper

¾ cup marinara sauce, store-bought
   or homemade

¾ cup part-skim shredded mozzarella
   cheese

¼ cup grated Parmesan cheese

Dried oregano to taste

10 cherry tomatoes, thinly sliced
   into rounds

HOW TO MAKE IT

Preheat the oven to 400°F. Mist a baking sheet with oil spray and set aside.

Cut off and discard both ends of the eggplant and then slice the eggplant into rounds about ½-inch thick. Arrange the eggplant slices in a single layer on the baking sheet.

Brush the tops of the eggplant slices with the olive oil and sprinkle with salt and pepper to taste. Bake for 20 minutes, or until the eggplant is soft and golden brown.

Top each slice with about 1 tablespoon of the marinara sauce and 1 tablespoon of the mozzarella cheese. Sprinkle the slices with the Parmesan cheese and oregano, and have fun making smiley faces with the cherry tomatoes and extra cheese. Bake for another 5 to 10 minutes, or until the cheese is hot and bubbly.

MINI BUT MIGHTY...

eggplant pizza perfection!

Flip the flap . . . it's pizza time!

DOWNWARD DOG
Strengthens your whole body.

ONE-IN-A-MELON FRUIT KEBABS

Makes about 3 kebabs

WHAT YOU'LL NEED

1 cup watermelon, cubed

1 peach, cubed

1 cup honeydew or cantaloupe, cubed

1 mango, cubed

Note: Swap in any other fresh fruits you like!

HOW TO MAKE IT

Carefully thread the fruit cubes onto wooden skewers, alternating between the four varieties. Enjoy immediately, or place in freezer for about an hour for an icy consistency.

Safety first: Have an adult help you build the kebabs, and be careful with the pointy tips. If you don't have wooden skewers, you can enjoy the cubed fruits in a fruit salad or use them as building blocks to make a pyramid.

SUPER SKEWERS:

flavorful fruit, packed with juicy goodness!

Check under the flap for your new favorite way to eat fruit!

FORWARD BEND POSE
Makes your back and legs more flexible.

YOU CAN

HERE ARE THE EIGHT YOGA POSES featured in this book, along with some notes about how to form each pose. One of the most important things when doing yoga is to focus on your breathing. As you move into each pose, inhale and exhale deeply and slowly through your nose. This calms you down and gives your brain and muscles the oxygen they need.

TRIANGLE POSE

With your legs wide apart, point your left foot forward and your right foot to the side. Stretch your left hand up in the air as high as you can, keeping your arm straight. Now slowly bend your body to the side, moving your right hand toward your right ankle. Keep your chest lifted and your back straight. Turn your head gently to look up at the fingertips of your left hand. Your body is now in the shape of a triangle! This pose makes the muscles in your back, hips, and thighs stronger, and can also help improve your balance.

DO YOGA!

LOTUS POSE

Sit down and stretch your legs out in front of you. Now cross your legs like a pretzel (*criss-cross-applesauce!*) and stretch the top of your head toward the sky so you are sitting up tall and straight. Rest your hands on your knees with your palms facing up. Close your eyes and focus on breathing deeply in and out through your nose. This pose is great for calming your mind; stretching your knees, ankles, and hips; and strengthening the muscles in your back.

PLANK POSE

Start on your hands and knees, with your shoulders lined up over your wrists. Shift your weight to your forearms as you pick up your feet to step back behind you, until your body is in one straight line. Hold steady for a few long breaths. Release the pose by coming down gently onto your knees. Great for strengthening all of your core muscles, including your abdomen, lower back, and chest.

WARRIOR II POSE

From a standing position, take a big step backward with one of your legs, and then turn your back foot so it is pointing away from your body. Now, bend your front knee until it's lined up over your ankle. Spread your arms wide like a T, so that one arm is above your front leg and the other is above your back leg. Turn your head gently to look over your front fingertips. You are now a warrior! This powerful pose makes the muscles in your legs and core stronger and helps stretch your legs and hips.

TREE POSE

Stand up tall and straight. Keep one foot on the ground and lift the other foot up, bending your lifted knee and turning it out to the side. Place the sole of your foot onto the leg that you are standing on, either on your ankle, calf, or thigh (but not your knee), depending on where you can best hold your balance. Next, bring your palms together over your head, with your fingertips pointing up. Do you feel like a tall tree? When you've finished, you can try the pose again, this time lifting up the other foot. This pose is perfect for practicing your balance.

CAT POSE

Begin on your hands and knees, with your hands lined up under your shoulders and your knees lined up under your hips. Breathe in deeply, and then, as you breathe out, arch your back like there's a big ball beneath your stomach. Gently relax your head so you're looking down at your knees. The cat pose is great for warming up your back and spine.

DOWNWARD DOG POSE

Start on your hands and knees, with your fingers spread out wide and your toes tucked under your feet. Slowly pull your hips up to the sky and straighten your arms and legs, so that your hands, bottom, and feet make an upside-down V. Gently relax your head so you're looking down at your legs. You're now in downward dog pose! This position helps make your entire body stronger, from your arms down to your feet, and also helps stretch your shoulders and spine.

FORWARD BEND POSE

Sit down with both of your legs stretched out straight in front of you. Take a breath in and, as you breathe out, bend forward and reach for your toes. If you can't touch them, that's okay—just stretch as far as you can! Take a few deep breaths in and out through your nose. Release the pose by slowly straightening your spine and relaxing your arms. The forward bend pose is a great way to make your back and legs more flexible.

Thank you to my dear friend—and talented, creative photographer—Bonnie Stephens, who magically turns healthy food into delicious-looking yogis. To the Abrams publishing group, in particular Meredith Mundy, Hana Anouk Nakamura, and Amy Vreeland, for handling every single detail with care and precision. Heartfelt thanks to my lead nutritionist, Rebecca Jay Forman, and to my editorial director, Donna Fennessy, for helping me every step of the way.

To Jane Dystel, Miriam Goderich, Jami Kandel, Ryan Nord, Robin Maizes, and my Nourish Snacks family for always believing in me and supporting me throughout each and every journey. Infinite thanks to Lucy Schaeffer for the incredible food photography, Leslie Orlandi for the gorgeous food styling, and to chef Jessie Levin for lending continuous assistance.

Hugs and kisses to my ginormous loving family: You guys are the apple to my peanut butter.

To my mom and dad, who always let me play with my food. —J.B.

To my wonderful, supportive family. And to my flexible, edible yogis . . . I say, "Namaste. You were delicious." —B.S.

Cataloging-in-Publication Data has been applied for and can be obtained from the Library of Congress.

ISBN 978-1-4197-3824-1

All text and all recipe photographs copyright © 2019 Joy Bauer
Food sculpture photographs copyright © 2019 Bonnie Stephens
Book design by Hana Anouk Nakamura

Printed and bound in China
10 9 8 7 6 5 4 3 2

Abrams Books for Young Readers are available at special discounts when purchased in quantity for premiums and promotions as well as fundraising or educational use. Special editions can also be created to specification. For details, contact specialsales@abramsbooks.com or the address below.

Abrams® is a registered trademark of Harry N. Abrams, Inc.

ABRAMS The Art of Books
195 Broadway, New York, NY 10007
abramsbooks.com